Comprehension Skills

INFERENCE

LEVEL

STECK-VAUGHN
COMPANY
A Subsidiary of National Education Corporation

Executive Editor:	Diane Sharpe
Project Editor:	Melinda Veatch
Design Coordinator:	Sharon Golden
Project Design:	Howard Adkins Communications
Cover Illustration:	Rhonda Childress
Photographs:	©David Young Wolff / PhotoEdit

ISBN 0-8114-7841-6

5 6 7 8 9 0 VP 96

Making an inference means making a guess. You can make this guess by putting together what you know and what you read or see. You will make inferences about the stories in this book.

You make inferences all the time. Look at the picture. Have you ever stood in front of a group? How do you think the girl in this picture feels? What helped you make this inference?

What Is an Inference?

An inference is a guess you make after thinking about what you already know. Suppose a friend invites you to a picnic. From what you know about picnics, you might infer that there will be food and drinks, and you will eat outside.

An author does not write every detail in a story. If every detail were told, a story would be long and boring. And the main point would be lost. Suppose you read, "Lynn went to a restaurant." The writer does not have to tell you what a restaurant is. You already know that it is a place where people go to eat a meal. From what you know, you might imagine that Lynn looked at a menu. Then a server took her order. By filling in these missing details, you could infer that Lynn went to the restaurant to eat. You can infer this by putting together what you read and what you already know.

Try It!

Read this story. Think about the facts in the story.

---◆---

Earthquakes can cause a lot of damage. This is especially true in places where the soil is loose and damp. An earthquake can turn loose, damp soil into thick mud. Buildings will sink or fall down. Many people may be hurt.

What can you infer? Write an inference on the line below.

You might have written something such as "An earthquake can harm a city." You can make this inference from what the story tells you about earthquakes and what you already know.

Practice Making Inferences

In units 1 through 12, you will be asked to answer the question "Which of these sentences is probably true?" Read the following story.

---◆---

Red-crowned cranes are beautiful birds. They are known for their trumpeting call. Half of these cranes live on an island in Japan. They live in marshes and are protected by law. But there are fewer than a thousand cranes left. They are in danger of disappearing.

 1. Which of these sentences is probably true?

    A. The Japanese don't care about these cranes.
    B. People in Japan want to help the cranes.
    C. Red-crowned cranes live in the desert.
    D. There are too many cranes in Japan.

Only one answer is a good choice. Read answer **B**. It is the best choice. The story says that these cranes are in danger of disappearing and that they are protected by law. From the story you can infer that people in Japan want to help these cranes.

Read the following story. Answer it on your own.

---◆---

Will was a baby and only knew a few words. One day he pointed to a dog and said, "Dog!" His mother praised him for learning a new word. The next day Will pointed to a cat and said, "Dog!" Later a squirrel ran by. Will pointed and shouted, "Dog!"

2. Which of these sentences is probably true?

    A. Will wanted his bottle.
    B. Will was afraid of dogs.
    C. Will thought that all small animals were dogs.
    D. Will liked cats better than squirrels.

To check your answer, turn to page 62.

More Practice Making Inferences

In units 13 through 25 of this book, you will do a new kind of exercise. Each story is followed by statements. Some of the statements are inferences. Others are facts. Decide whether each statement is an inference or a fact. Read this story.

◆

Ben moved from England to Maine. In England he was taught to stand up when answering a question. So in his new class, he stood up when the teacher called on him. Some of the other students laughed at him. After class the teacher told him that he could stay in his seat when she called on him.

Fact	Inference	
○	●	**1.** **A.** Ben was a polite person.
●	○	**B.** Ben moved from England to Maine.
○	●	**C.** The teacher wanted to help Ben.
●	○	**D.** Some students laughed at Ben.

You can find statements **B** and **D** in the story. So they are facts. We can infer from the way he acts that Ben is a polite person. But this isn't stated in the story. So **A** is an inference. We can guess from the teacher's actions that she wanted to help Ben. So **C** is also an inference.

Read this story. Mark your answers.

◆

Pigs are smart. They can learn many tricks. They can fetch sticks, dance, and tumble. It takes a pig less time than a dog to learn tricks. Pigs like people and are very curious. Pigs can even learn to open gates and locks.

Fact	Inference	
○	○	**2.** **A.** Pigs can learn to open locks.
○	○	**B.** Pigs can learn many tricks.
○	○	**C.** Pigs are smarter than dogs.
○	○	**D.** Pigs are curious.

To check your answers, turn to page 62.

How to Use This Book

Read the stories in this book. Answer the question after each story. You can check your answers yourself. If you wish, tear out pages 59 through 62. Find the unit you want to check. Fold the answer page on the dotted line to show the correct unit. Line up the answer page with the answers you wrote. Write the number of correct answers in the score box at the top of the page.

You can have fun with inferences. Turn to pages 56 through 58 and work through "Think and Apply."

Remember

In this book there are two kinds of exercises. In units 1 through 12, you are asked, "Which of these sentences is probably true?" From what you read and what you know, you can choose the best answer. In units 13 through 25, you are asked to decide whether each statement is a fact or an inference.

Hints for Better Reading

◆ As you read keep in mind the difference between facts and inferences.

◆ Think about the facts in the story. Think about what you already know. Make an inference by putting together what you know and what you've read.

Challenge Yourself

Read each story. Write one more inference you can make about each story.

1. Joe was a teen-age chess player. He thought he was a pretty good player. So he decided to play more than a hundred people at once. Just twenty people showed up to play him, though. And eighteen of those beat him, including a small boy.

2. It was 1865. A train moved slowly from town to town. It was going from Washington, D.C., to Illinois. The body of Abraham Lincoln was on the train. People stood on both sides of the tracks in each town. They stood quietly as the train passed. Their eyes were full of tears.

3. John loved to fish. He went fishing anytime he could. The weather was very hot and dry. John sat on the shore, thinking about catching fish. But the fish just would not bite. All day John waited patiently. He was hungry and thirsty. But even as the sun went down, he did not move.

4. The dog hurried home. It had a juicy bone in its mouth. It could hardly wait to get home to enjoy its meal. As the dog crossed a stream, it stopped in the middle of the bridge. It looked in the still water. There it saw another dog with a bone in its mouth. The dog thought it could bark and scare away the other dog. Then it could have that bone, too. But as the dog barked, its bone fell in the water. Then the other dog disappeared.

5. In 1659 the country of Sweden made some new money. These metal coins were quite large. And they were hard to use. Each one weighed more than thirty pounds. They were the largest coins in history.

_____ **1.** Which of these sentences is probably true?

    A. Joe wasn't a good chess player.
    B. Some of Joe's chess pieces were lost.
    C. Joe didn't try to win, because he was tired.
    D. The other players were sick and couldn't come.

_____ **2.** Which of these sentences is probably true?

    A. The people did not like trains.
    B. The train didn't make very much noise.
    C. The people were sad that Lincoln had died.
    D. The train had never been to Illinois before.

_____ **3.** Which of these sentences is probably true?

    A. There were no fish in the water.
    B. John wanted to stay until he caught a fish.
    C. Other people were fishing at the pond.
    D. John went home early for dinner.

_____ **4.** Which of these sentences is probably true?

    A. The dog wasn't hungry.
    B. It was a rainy day.
    C. The bone was not heavy.
    D. The dog was greedy.

_____ **5.** Which of these sentences is probably true?

    A. The coins were not very pretty.
    B. The Swedish people stopped using the coins.
    C. Other countries started making large coins, too.
    D. The Swedish people did not like history.

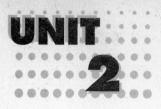

1. The village people chose a boy to guard the sheep. It was an important job. If a wolf came near, the boy was supposed to call the people in the village. Then they would come to help him. The boy watched the sheep for a little while. Then he decided to have some fun. He cried out loudly, "Wolf! Wolf!" The people rushed out to fight the wolf. When they arrived the boy was laughing at them. There was no wolf.

2. Huck Finn had a friend named Jim, but Jim was a slave. Jim was always sad, and he didn't smile very often. Huck decided to help Jim escape to freedom.

3. In the 1950s golf was a new sport in Japan. Many people liked the game. The golfers practiced and practiced. They tried to hit the small, hard balls across the golf course grass. But those who played golf were in great danger. In fact, people on the golf course had to wear hard hats for their own safety.

4. The young donkey stopped in the middle of the road. Ted and Sally jumped down from their cart and looked at the brown animal. First Ted yelled at the donkey, but it would not move. Then Sally tapped it with a stick, but still nothing happened. Ted even used a carrot to make the donkey go on, but it would not. Giving up, Ted and Sally sat down by the road to wait.

5. People once thought that frogs could help make sick people well. They put a dead frog in a box. Then they tied the box around the sick person's neck. As the frog started to smell worse and worse, the sick person was supposed to get better.

_____ **1.** Which of these sentences is probably true?
    A. Everyone thought the joke was funny.
    B. Several of the sheep got lost.
    C. The people were angry at the boy.
    D. The boy was very kind.

_____ **2.** Which of these sentences is probably true?
    A. Jim did not like being a slave.
    B. Huck wanted Jim to be his slave.
    C. Jim didn't trust Huck very much.
    D. Huck thought Jim needed new clothes.

_____ **3.** Which of these sentences is probably true?
    A. Playing golf in the United States is not very safe.
    B. At first the golfers in Japan didn't play very well.
    C. People in Japan also played football.
    D. Golfers in Japan were often hit by lightning.

_____ **4.** Which of these sentences is probably true?
    A. The road was bumpy and full of holes.
    B. The donkey wouldn't give in easily.
    C. Ted and Sally were old and tired.
    D. The donkey was very hungry.

_____ **5.** Which of these sentences is probably true?
    A. Most frogs have a nice smell.
    B. Dead frogs are still used today.
    C. Healthy people wore live frogs.
    D. Sick people no longer wear dead frogs.

1. A pet store owner in Maine noticed a strange thing. He found that he could tell when the country was having good times or bad. He looked at what kind of dogs people wanted to buy. People bought small dogs when they had enough money. People bought big dogs when they felt sad or needed protection.

2. Ichabod Crane listened politely as the old man spoke. His voice was full of fear. He told Crane about a ghost. It was called the Headless Horseman. The ghost scared people who entered a place called Sleepy Hollow after dark. Crane laughed to himself as he listened to the story. That night Crane took a short cut through Sleepy Hollow. Before he knew it, the ghost was chasing him.

3. The cowbird does not build a nest of its own. The mother cowbird lays her eggs in the nest of another bird. Then the cowbird leaves the eggs. She hopes the other bird will take care of her babies when they hatch.

4. The game was almost over. The Mudville team was losing, but Casey was the next batter. He was the best hitter on the team. The Mudville crowd roared as the pitcher threw one strike, then another. If Casey missed one more pitch, he would strike out. The pitcher threw again, and the Mudville crowd grew very quiet. Casey walked away from the plate.

5. Long ago, farmers watched animals to see when snow was coming. They thought snow would fall if a cat sneezed. Others felt that a dog with more fleas than usual was a sign of coming snow. Others watched for birds sitting high in the trees. That was a warning of snow, too.

_____ **1.** Which of these sentences is probably true?
- **A.** People bought big dogs during bad times.
- **B.** Pet store owners don't like dogs.
- **C.** People bought big dogs during good times.
- **D.** Dogs make better pets than cats do.

_____ **2.** Which of these sentences is probably true?
- **A.** The old man lived in Sleepy Hollow.
- **B.** Crane did not believe the man's story.
- **C.** Sleepy Hollow was far away.
- **D.** Crane liked to be scared.

_____ **3.** Which of these sentences is probably true?
- **A.** The cowbird is lazy.
- **B.** Nests are hard to build.
- **C.** The cowbird is very caring.
- **D.** Baby cowbirds eat much food.

_____ **4.** Which of these sentences is probably true?
- **A.** Casey hit the ball over the fence.
- **B.** The crowd forgot to cheer.
- **C.** Casey's team won the game.
- **D.** On the last pitch, Casey struck out.

_____ **5.** Which of these sentences is probably true?
- **A.** Farmers were happy when heavy snow fell.
- **B.** Most farmers enjoyed skiing and climbing mountains.
- **C.** Farmers thought birds could tell when snow was coming.
- **D.** Farmers did not have many dogs or cats.

1. Jim Smiley thought he was smarter than anyone else. Jim liked to be in contests, and he almost always won them. One day a new man arrived in town. This stranger offered to have a frog-jumping contest with Jim. Jim agreed and said he would find a good frog for the stranger. While Jim was gone, the stranger tied small weights to the legs of Jim's frog. Soon Jim returned with the stranger's frog.

2. May Pierstorff took a strange trip in 1914. May's parents wanted her to visit her grandparents. They lived one hundred miles away. But a train ticket for May cost too much money. So her parents sent her by mail! It cost them 53 cents. May passed all the rules for being mailed. So May rode in the train mail car. She arrived safely.

3. One day Ann heard her friend Tom talking. Tom was telling everybody how smart his dog was. Tom said his dog could do tricks and could even ride a bicycle. But Ann knew that Tom's dog was just like any other dog. So Ann just smiled as Tom went on talking.

4. Dirty Dan never played fairly. He would do anything to win. One day he was playing tennis against Sweet Sue. When Dan walked out on the court, the crowd yelled "Boo!"

5. Fingernails grow faster on the right hand of people who are right-handed. The nails grow faster on the left hand of left-handed people. They grow faster in the day than at night. Ray has to trim the nails on his left hand more than the ones on his right hand.

_____ **1.** Which of these sentences is probably true?

    A. Jim's frog won the contest.

    B. The stranger's frog won the contest.

    C. Jim's frog jumped farther than it ever had.

    D. The frog tricked the stranger.

_____ **2.** Which of these sentences is probably true?

    A. May's parents wanted to save money.

    B. May didn't want to visit her grandparents.

    C. May was lost in the mail.

    D. May tried to walk to her grandparents' house.

_____ **3.** Which of these sentences is probably true?

    A. Ann didn't understand Tom's story.

    B. Tom wanted to make Ann mad at him.

    C. Ann didn't want to hurt Tom's feelings.

    D. Tom had two dogs and a cat.

_____ **4.** Which of these sentences is probably true?

    A. A skunk walked out on the court with Dan.

    B. The crowd wanted to scare Dan.

    C. Dan looked like last year's winning player.

    D. The crowd did not like Dan.

_____ **5.** Which of these sentences is probably true?

    A. Ray is a right-handed person.

    B. Painted nails grow very slowly.

    C. Ray is a left-handed person.

    D. At night Ray's nails grow quickly.

1. Shannon wanted to buy the doll she saw in the magazine. She begged her mother to give her the money. Shannon carefully wrote a letter to order the doll. Then she sent the letter in the mail. For weeks Shannon waited. Each day she hoped the doll would arrive. She knew the doll would be the best thing she had ever owned. At last the package arrived. But when Shannon opened the box, she found the doll broken into pieces.

2. The army ants of South America eat insects. These ants travel in groups. They sweep across the land in a dark bunch. People leave their homes for a while if they are in the ants' path.

3. Long ago in China, people had a strange idea about the world. They thought the world sat on the back of a giant frog. When the frog moved, the weather changed.

4. One day Sam found a library book under his bed. He realized he was late in taking it back. Sam decided to return the book the next day. But the next day, he could not find the book. Two days later Sam found the book again, so he hurried to the library. But when he arrived, there was a sign on the door. So he walked home again with the book in his hand.

5. King James had a plan. He wanted to make London the center of the silk business. He knew that silkworms made silk. People would pay lots of money for pretty silk clothes. The king planted a black mulberry tree at his palace. He told others in the land to plant the trees, too. He knew that silk worms ate many mulberry leaves. But there was one thing the king did not know. Silkworms would only eat the leaves of the white mulberry tree.

_____ **1.** Which of these sentences is probably true?

    A. Shannon cried when she opened the box.

    B. Getting the doll made Shannon happy.

    C. Shannon knew the doll would be broken.

    D. Shannon thought the broken doll was funny.

_____ **2.** Which of these sentences is probably true?

    A. People are really insects.

    B. The ants eat animals.

    C. People return after the ants pass.

    D. The ants ride on trains.

_____ **3.** Which of these sentences is probably true?

    A. Long ago the world was smaller.

    B. China was filled with small frogs.

    C. Long ago the weather was different.

    D. The Chinese people were trying to explain the weather.

_____ **4.** Which of these sentences is probably true?

    A. Sam didn't like the book very much.

    B. The book could move by itself.

    C. Sam did not know where the library was.

    D. When Sam went to the library, it was closed.

_____ **5.** Which of these sentences is probably true?

    A. Silkworms ate the black mulberry leaves.

    B. The king's plan didn't work out.

    C. London became the center of the silk business.

    D. The king moved to a new palace.

1. The day was sunny and hot. Ava stood happily at the side of the swimming pool. She thought about the clear, blue water. Then she jumped in. But as she began swimming, she started shaking, and her skin began to turn blue.

2. When Louisa May Alcott was four, she had a birthday party. Many children were invited. Each child was supposed to get a small cake as a treat. Louisa handed out the cakes. She soon noticed that there were not enough cakes for everyone. One little girl was left in line, and there was only one cake left. Louisa wanted the cake for herself. But she smiled and gave the last cake to her friend.

3. Nick sat trembling behind the couch as a storm roared outside. Lightning flashed and thunder rumbled. Each time the thunder rolled, Nick screamed loudly. Nick's dad tried to get the boy to come out, but Nick would not move.

4. Six people in Maine came up with a plan. They wanted to help their high school basketball team. They decided to bounce a basketball to the next town. Their team had its next game there. The December weather was cold and wet. But the six people did not let the bad weather stop them. They bounced the ball twenty miles to the next town. When they arrived they learned that the game would not be played. The weather was too bad.

5. After school on Thursday, Fred played video games. That night he watched TV and then read some magazines in his room. The next morning Fred walked slowly to his classroom. When the teacher passed out the test, the class began working. Fred stared at the questions. To him they seemed to be in a different language.

_____ **1.** Which of these sentences is probably true?

    A. The water was very hot.

    B. Ava forgot to wear her coat.

    C. The water was very cold.

    D. Ava didn't know how to swim.

_____ **2.** Which of these sentences is probably true?

    A. The last little girl wanted two cakes.

    B. Louisa was kind and sharing.

    C. The last little girl was not hungry.

    D. Louisa was not very friendly.

_____ **3.** Which of these sentences is probably true?

    A. Storms made Nick's dad afraid.

    B. Nick liked to play hide and seek.

    C. Nick's dad made him feel better.

    D. Nick was afraid of thunder and lightning.

_____ **4.** Which of these sentences is probably true?

    A. The six people were disappointed when they arrived.

    B. The basketball players didn't like the six people.

    C. Bouncing the ball in the cold was fun.

    D. The six people were glad no one showed up.

_____ **5.** Which of these sentences is probably true?

    A. The teacher passed out the wrong test.

    B. Fred did not do well on the test.

    C. The test was printed upside down.

    D. Fred did not need to study.

1. When his mother closed the door, Adam felt all alone. Adam was glad that the light by his bed was still on. Outside his window dark shadows danced in the night sky. He checked under his bed. Then he pulled the covers over his head. At last he was able to close his eyes and fall asleep.

2. Bill Stanton found a skunk in his garage. He asked the city of Chicago for help. He wanted to get rid of the skunk, but the city would not help him. So Bill bought a trap to catch the skunk himself. Then he learned he had broken the law several times. First he had brought a trap into the city. Then he had trapped an animal without the city's permission. The city laws stated that he could not keep the skunk in his garage. But they also said he could not kill the skunk or let it go free, either!

3. Tom Sawyer stared at the long, wooden fence. His aunt had ordered him to paint it. But just the thought of all that work made Tom tired. Then he had a wonderful idea. As he began to paint, he played like he was having lots of fun. Other boys arrived to watch. They wanted to have fun, too. Soon Tom had all the other boys doing his work for him.

4. During World War II, there wasn't enough rubber. So wooden tires for cars were tested. The wooden tires worked very well on smooth roads. But they cracked easily when they hit a hole.

5. The sport of softball began as indoor baseball. The first game of softball was played on a cold day in November 1887. It took place in a Chicago boat club. The men used an old boxing glove for a ball and a broomstick for a bat.

SCORE

_____ **1.** Which of these sentences is probably true?

    A. Adam felt safe when his mom was in the room.

    B. Going to sleep was easy for Adam.

    C. The shadows outside did not scare Adam.

    D. Adam thought his mother was under the bed.

_____ **2.** Which of these sentences is probably true?

    A. The skunk became Bill's best friend.

    B. Bill didn't know what to do with the skunk.

    C. The skunk was moved to the city leaders' office.

    D. Bill was glad the skunk was in his garage.

_____ **3.** Which of these sentences is probably true?

    A. Working hard was fun for Tom.

    B. Tom didn't like fences.

    C. Tom's aunt painted the fence.

    D. Tom was a very tricky boy.

_____ **4.** Which of these sentences is probably true?

    A. Today wooden tires are still used.

    B. Making wooden tires was a good idea.

    C. Wooden tires did not replace rubber tires.

    D. The people who made wooden tires got rich.

_____ **5.** Which of these sentences is probably true?

    A. The men wanted to play baseball in the winter.

    B. Real baseballs cost a lot of money in 1887.

    C. The men didn't know how to play baseball.

    D. People first played softball outside.

1. Troy's dad had told him to come straight home after school. Troy was supposed to help his dad wash the car. But after school Troy talked to some friends for a while. On the way home, he stopped at the park to play basketball. When Troy finally got home, he saw that the car was already washed.

2. A town in California needed a footbridge. But the town leaders couldn't decide how to build it. They didn't know how much money to spend. One company said it would build the bridge for seven million dollars. The leaders talked about it for months. At last two boys decided to act. They built the bridge by themselves!

3. One day Kim went to the mall with her dad. First they visited a shoe store. Kim's dad just looked at the different shoes, but Kim bought two pairs. Then they decided to go to a toy store. There Kim bought a game and a soccer ball. Kim's dad soon got tired. He was ready to go home, but Kim wanted to look in several more stores.

4. Pedro Vinales was not very good at his job. He was a horse racer. He rode horses in more than three hundred races. But he never won a race. One day he had a good idea. He quit his job at the age of 28.

5. When Benjamin Franklin was a boy, he and his friends had an idea. They wanted to build a small dock to walk on. That way they could fish in the middle of the lake. They found a place to build it by the edge of the water. But they needed stones to build the dock. They found a pile of stones and started to work. Later the boys were surprised to learn that the stones had been gathered to build part of a new house.

_____ **1.** Which of these sentences is probably true?

    A. His dad didn't mind that Troy was late.

    B. Troy got in trouble for being late.

    C. His dad was glad that Troy had a good time.

    D. Troy had a special treat for supper.

_____ **2.** Which of these sentences is probably true?

    A. The boys liked to spend their own money.

    B. Building bridges was the boys' job.

    C. After one week the boys had finished the bridge.

    D. The boys got tired of waiting for the town's plan.

_____ **3.** Which of these sentences is probably true?

    A. Kim's family was very poor.

    B. Kim didn't like malls.

    C. Kim's dad was mean to her.

    D. Kim loved to go shopping.

_____ **4.** Which of these sentences is probably true?

    A. Pedro got tired of losing.

    B. Quitting his job was hard for Pedro.

    C. Pedro did not like horses.

    D. Racing horses is an easy job.

_____ **5.** Which of these sentences is probably true?

    A. The workers helped the boys build the dock.

    B. Franklin lied about taking the stones.

    C. The workers were angry with the boys.

    D. The boys did not use the stones.

1. At last the time came for Amy to give her report. She had to stand in front of the whole class and tell them about spiders. As she stood up, she dropped her report. The pages scattered all across the floor. Amy could feel everyone staring at her as she picked up the mess. Finally she reached the front of the room. She looked out at the class. Amy could feel her face turning red. She tried to speak, but no words would come out of her mouth.

2. The speed limit on the road was 30 miles per hour. But drivers always went faster than that. The neighbors who lived on the road were angry about the speeders. So they talked to the city leaders. The leaders soon took action. They raised the speed limit to 35 miles per hour.

3. It was a cold day, and Ali stared at the white snow that covered the sidewalk. He knew he had a lot of shoveling to do. He was supposed to clean off the whole sidewalk. Out in the street, Ali's friends were pulling their sleds. Ali knew they were going to have fun sledding down the hill. They called for him to come, but Ali just waved. As they walked away, Ali slowly started to shovel.

4. If you are sick and you cough or sneeze on someone, that person could get sick, too. But it is not really a good idea to stop yourself from sneezing. If you do, you could pull a muscle in your face. You could also make your nose bleed.

5. Animals lose heat through their tails and ears. Animals that live in warm places have bigger ears and tails than those that live in cold places. A desert fox has long ears. But an arctic fox has short ears.

_____ **1.** Which of these sentences is probably true?

    A. Amy was in the wrong class.

    B. The class was afraid of Amy.

    C. Talking in front of people was hard for Amy.

    D. Amy knew nothing about spiders.

_____ **2.** Which of these sentences is probably true?

    A. The neighbors disliked the new speed limit.

    B. The neighbors were glad the leaders took action.

    C. After hearing the leaders' decision, the neighbors moved away.

    D. Drivers started going 30 miles per hour.

_____ **3.** Which of these sentences is probably true?

    A. Ali would rather work than play.

    B. The other children didn't like Ali.

    C. Ali loved to shovel snow.

    D. When Ali had a job to do, he did it.

_____ **4.** Which of these sentences is probably true?

    A. Sneezing makes your nose bleed.

    B. Stopping a sneeze could be harmful.

    C. You can get over a cold by not sneezing.

    D. Sneezing is good exercise for your face.

_____ **5.** Which of these sentences is probably true?

    A. Big ears help keep animals cool.

    B. Desert foxes need big ears to hear well.

    C. Animals with big ears eat healthier food.

    D. Arctic foxes need long ears.

1. Bob Hope was playing golf with a friend. His friend missed an easy shot. The angry friend threw his golf club into the tall grass. Bob secretly got the golf club back and started using it himself. Bob hit the ball a long way with his friend's club. The friend thought Bob's golf club was very good. He offered to buy it for fifty dollars. Bob sold the man the club he had just thrown away. Later Bob told his friend what had happened.

2. Jo's mom was in the hospital. She had just had a new baby. Jo had seen the little thing with its wrinkled skin and its funny face. Jo was excited to have a new brother. But she was worried that her parents might not love her anymore.

3. The President was coming to visit the small town. Everyone was very excited. All the people worked hard to clean up their town. They mowed the grass and swept the sidewalks. They fixed up the old houses. They even painted the water tower.

4. Morgan's dad had gone to have the car fixed. Morgan couldn't believe how much old stuff was piled up in the garage. Morgan stared at it for a while, and then he knew what he had to do. The garage was filled with noise and dust that afternoon. But when Morgan's dad arrived home with the car, the garage was as clean as could be.

5. Samuel Clemens grew up near the Mississippi River. As a boy he played by the river for hours. He watched the water change colors as the sun moved through the sky. When he got older, Clemens got a job as a riverboat pilot. He later changed his name to Mark Twain. His new name came from a saying that riverboat pilots used. The saying told how deep the water was.

_____ **1.** Which of these sentences is probably true?

    A. Bob decided to keep his friend's golf club.

    B. Bob's friend felt silly for buying back his own club.

    C. Bob used the money to open a golf shop.

    D. Bob's friend never played golf again.

_____ **2.** Which of these sentences is probably true?

    A. Jo's parents needed to tell her they could love two children.

    B. Jo did not like wrinkles or funny faces.

    C. Jo's mother was at home.

    D. Jo wanted a dog instead of a new baby brother.

_____ **3.** Which of these sentences is probably true?

    A. The President was moving to the town.

    B. The people were trying to fool the President.

    C. The President only liked big towns.

    D. The people wanted their town to look nice.

_____ **4.** Which of these sentences is probably true?

    A. Morgan liked fixing cars.

    B. Morgan's father had been sick.

    C. Morgan was a hard worker.

    D. Morgan's father liked dirty garages.

_____ **5.** Which of these sentences is probably true?

    A. Clemens loved the river.

    B. The other pilots didn't like Clemens.

    C. Clemens could not swim.

    D. The river always looked the same.

1. Jim carefully lifted the eggs from their box. He handed two eggs to his mother. Then Jim measured a cup of milk, being careful not to spill any. He rubbed the cake pan with butter and watched as his mother poured in the batter. Then Jim and his mother cleaned up.

2. Marion Morrison was born in 1907. He grew up in a small town in Iowa. When he got older, he moved to California. There he began to make movies. He often played the part of a tough cowboy. He decided to change his name. His new name was John Wayne. He soon became a famous star.

3. Jan was always playing basketball. In fact, she almost never left the basketball court. Jan started practicing early every morning. As the sun went down, Jan was still bouncing the basketball.

4. Nan was helping her uncle on the farm. He was loading the truck with hay for the cows. Nan's uncle threw a rope over the bales of hay. He told Nan to tie the rope carefully. But Nan only tied a loose knot. Then she hurried off to get a cool drink.

5. When Babe Ruth was a boy, he was very poor. He had a lot of problems. He often got in fights with other boys, and many times he lost. At last he was sent to St. Mary's School. There he met Brother Gilbert. Brother Gilbert discovered the one thing that would keep Babe out of trouble. He introduced Babe to baseball.

_____ **1.** Which of these sentences is probably true?
   A. Jim was a good helper.
   B. Jim's mother was a bad cook.
   C. Jim was hungry.
   D. Jim's mother was lazy.

_____ **2.** Which of these sentences is probably true?
   A. Marion's mother was named Mrs. Wayne.
   B. Marion changed his name to Sam.
   C. Marion's father was a tough cowboy.
   D. Marion thought John Wayne was a better name for a cowboy.

_____ **3.** Which of these sentences is probably true?
   A. Jan slept at the basketball court.
   B. Tennis was very important to Jan.
   C. Jan wanted to be a great basketball player.
   D. The basketball was too big to bounce inside.

_____ **4.** Which of these sentences is probably true?
   A. All the cool drinks were already gone.
   B. The rope tightened itself.
   C. The knot came untied.
   D. The cool drink made Nan sick.

_____ **5.** Which of these sentences is probably true?
   A. Baseball got Babe Ruth in trouble.
   B. Babe Ruth loved playing baseball.
   C. Baseball made Babe Ruth poor.
   D. Babe Ruth liked fighting more than playing baseball.

1. During World War II, young Anne Frank had a hard life. Her family had to hide from the German soldiers. They stayed in one small room. Anne was afraid day after day. To make herself feel better, she wrote about her feelings. One day she wrote, "In spite of everything, I still believe that people are really good at heart."

2. Jack walked slowly toward town, pulling his cow behind him. Jack and his mother were very poor. He was supposed to sell the cow for money to buy food. Along the way Jack met a funny little man. The man offered to trade some magic beans for Jack's cow. The man said the beans could make Jack happy. So Jack traded the cow for the beans.

3. When he was a boy, George Washington Carver had a garden. He loved to study the plants and flowers growing there. He knew how to make the flowers bloom. George could also cure sick plants. People began to call him the "plant doctor."

4. Greyfriars Bobby was a dog. He belonged to a policeman named Jock Gray. Bobby and Jock were great friends. When Jock died Bobby watched over the ground where Jock was buried. Bobby stayed close to the grave until he died.

5. Orville and Wilbur Wright loved to build things. When they were small, the brothers made paper toys that would fly. When they got older, they opened a bicycle shop. One day they thought about the flying toys they had made. They started trying to build a flying machine. They studied birds flying and made many models. At last their machine was complete. In 1903 Orville climbed into the machine and took off. Wilbur smiled with pride.

_____ **1.** Which of these sentences is probably true?

    A. Hiding in the little room was fun for Anne.

    B. Anne tried to think about the good things in life.

    C. Writing in the notebook was scary for Anne.

    D. Anne didn't think she had any problems.

_____ **2.** Which of these sentences is probably true?

    A. Jack did not like the cow.

    B. The cow wanted to go with the man.

    C. Jack believed in magic.

    D. The man was Jack's friend.

_____ **3.** Which of these sentences is probably true?

    A. George became a plant scientist later in life.

    B. The neighbors didn't like George's garden.

    C. George chopped down all the plants.

    D. His mother called George the "animal doctor."

_____ **4.** Which of these sentences is probably true?

    A. Bobby couldn't find his way home.

    B. Jock had been good to Bobby.

    C. Bobby never got hungry.

    D. Jock didn't have many friends.

_____ **5.** Which of these sentences is probably true?

    A. Their flying machine could fly.

    B. The Wright brothers fought a lot.

    C. Birds scared the Wright brothers.

    D. The Wright brothers loved flying.

1. Shoes were not always made differently for right and left feet. For hundreds of years, shoemakers made shoes to fit either foot. After shoes were worn for a while, the leather would stretch to fit the right or left foot. Around 1850 special sewing machines made it easier to produce shoes. Several years after that, shoes were made for each foot.

2. Jason and Josh were neighbors. They rode their bikes to school together every day. Josh got a new bike for his birthday. Jason wished he had a new bike, too. One day Josh left his bike in the yard. When he came back, it was gone.

3. Jenna sat alone at the lunch table. It was her first day at the new school. Katie, a girl in Jenna's class, was sitting at another table with her friends. She noticed Jenna eating lunch by herself. Katie walked over to the table where Jenna was sitting.

4. People have been eating cheese for over 4,000 years. Cheese is made from milk. As it turns to cheese, hard spots form in the milk. When the liquid is taken out, the cheese becomes even harder. The cheese is then allowed to *age*. This means it has to sit for a while before it's ready. Sometimes the cheese is ready to be eaten in two weeks. For other types of cheese, aging takes up to two years.

5. Lynn looked at a bag of candy on the table. She heard her mother's voice calling from another room, "We'll be eating in half an hour. Don't spoil your dinner." Lynn quietly walked over to the table. She grabbed a piece of candy and put it in her mouth.

Fact	Inference		
○	○	**1.** **A.**	Shoes stretched to fit each foot.
○	○	**B.**	Shoes were made of stretchy material.
○	○	**C.**	Leather can stretch.
○	○	**D.**	Shoes were made to fit either foot.

Fact	Inference		
○	○	**2.** **A.**	Jason wanted a new bike.
○	○	**B.**	Josh and Jason rode to school together.
○	○	**C.**	Jason took Josh's bike.
○	○	**D.**	Josh and Jason were neighbors.

Fact	Inference		
○	○	**3.** **A.**	Katie cared how Jenna felt.
○	○	**B.**	It was Jenna's first day at school.
○	○	**C.**	Katie walked to Jenna's table.
○	○	**D.**	Jenna was lonely.

Fact	Inference		
○	○	**4.** **A.**	Cheese is made from milk.
○	○	**B.**	There are different kinds of cheeses.
○	○	**C.**	Aging cheese can take two years.
○	○	**D.**	Cheese hardens when liquid is removed.

Fact	Inference		
○	○	**5.** **A.**	Lynn took a piece of candy.
○	○	**B.**	No one knew Lynn ate the candy.
○	○	**C.**	Lynn heard her mother.
○	○	**D.**	Lynn's mother was cooking.

1. Have you ever caught fireflies on a warm summer night? Fireflies are interesting little insects. They make light with their bodies. But the light is not hot. Fireflies use their lights to send signals to other fireflies.

2. A long time ago, no one knew that dinosaurs had ever lived. But in 1822 an English woman found a large tooth. In a few years, other parts of these large reptiles known as dinosaurs were found.

3. William loved to go fishing. His grandfather had promised to take him on Saturday. That morning William packed a lunch and got his fishing pole ready. But about an hour before it was time to go, the phone rang. His grandfather said he was not feeling well and couldn't take William fishing. William was disappointed, but decided to make his grandfather a get-well card.

4. Long ago, people gathered wild plants and hunted wild animals for food. At first people hunted only small animals. Later, they learned ways of catching larger animals. Half a million years ago, people learned to make fire. Before that they had to take burning wood from fires that had started naturally. When people learned to make their own fires, they began to cook some of their food.

5. It had been raining all day. Maria splashed through a puddle on her way home from school. As she came to her house, her dad opened the door. Maria quickly took off her raincoat. "Look, Maria," he said. "There's a surprise for you." A plate of Maria's favorite cookies was on the kitchen table.

Fact	Inference		
○	○	**1.**	**A.** Fireflies come out in summer.
○	○		**B.** The light of fireflies is not hot.
○	○		**C.** Fireflies send signals with their lights.
○	○		**D.** Fireflies can only send signals at night.

Fact	Inference		
○	○	**2.**	**A.** Dinosaurs lived before 1822.
○	○		**B.** Dinosaur bones were first found in England.
○	○		**C.** A tooth was the first dinosaur bone found.
○	○		**D.** Dinosaurs were reptiles.

Fact	Inference		
○	○	**3.**	**A.** William was a caring person.
○	○		**B.** William loved to go fishing.
○	○		**C.** William loved his grandfather.
○	○		**D.** William's grandfather was sick.

Fact	Inference		
○	○	**4.**	**A.** People hunted wild animals.
○	○		**B.** Large animals were hard to catch.
○	○		**C.** Fire was important to early people.
○	○		**D.** Some food was cooked over a fire.

Fact	Inference		
○	○	**5.**	**A.** Maria took off her raincoat.
○	○		**B.** It was a rainy day.
○	○		**C.** Maria walked through a puddle.
○	○		**D.** Maria's dad made cookies for her.

1. George Bidder was different from most boys his age. He was a whiz at math. When he was asked to work a math problem, he could do it in his head. Once he was told a 43-digit number backward. Right away he was able to switch it around in his head and say it forward in its correct order. He could even remember the number an hour later!

2. The city was full of people on their way home. Buses, trucks, cars, and taxis crowded the streets. Mark was in a hurry to catch the bus. As he ran up to the bus stop, the bus roared away. Mark sat down on a nearby bench and frowned.

3. Sarah had not studied for the science test. Her friend Beth always did very well in science. Sarah sat beside Beth in class. When Mrs. Banes began passing out the science test, Sarah leaned over to Beth. "Write big so I can see," she whispered. Later, Mrs. Banes called the two girls to her desk.

4. Robert Fulton built the first steamboat. His first try did not go very well. The boat sank to the bottom of the river. It was very heavy. A few years later, in 1807, he tried again. This time his boat, *The Clermont*, made a successful trip down the Hudson River in New York.

5. Drew's team was tied with the other soccer team. The game was almost over. Drew had scored all the goals in the game so far. His friend Brian had never scored a goal. As Drew ran up the field, he saw that Brian was in a great position to kick the ball into the goal. Drew quickly kicked the ball to Brian.

Fact	Inference		
○	○	**1.**	**A.** George worked math problems in his head.
○	○		**B.** Math was George's favorite subject.
○	○		**C.** George was a math whiz.
○	○		**D.** People thought George was very smart.

Fact	Inference		
○	○	**2.**	**A.** Mark ran to catch the bus.
○	○		**B.** Mark was angry he missed the bus.
○	○		**C.** The city streets were crowded.
○	○		**D.** Mark was on his way home.

Fact	Inference		
○	○	**3.**	**A.** Sarah had not studied.
○	○		**B.** The girls were caught cheating.
○	○		**C.** Beth did well in science.
○	○		**D.** Sarah whispered to Beth.

Fact	Inference		
○	○	**4.**	**A.** Robert Fulton did not give up easily.
○	○		**B.** Fulton's boat was called *The Clermont*.
○	○		**C.** *The Clermont* did not sink.
○	○		**D.** The first boat was very heavy.

Fact	Inference		
○	○	**5.**	**A.** Drew wanted Brian to make a goal.
○	○		**B.** Drew was a thoughtful person.
○	○		**C.** Drew was a good soccer player.
○	○		**D.** Brian had never scored a goal.

1. It gets much hotter and much colder on the moon than here on Earth. At noon the temperature is four times higher on the moon than on Earth. For two weeks the moon stays dark all day long. This is called lunar night. At that time it is four times colder than on Earth.

2. Miguel kicked the rocks in front of his feet. He had been excited about going to the rodeo. He wanted to see the cowboys do tricks. But now his mother wanted him to finish his farm work first. He slowly walked to the barn to water the horses. Then his brother's friend Ravon drove up in a truck. "How would you like a ride to the rodeo?" he asked.

3. Mount St. Helens is a volcano in Washington. In 1980 it erupted for the first time in over one hundred years. Fire and melting rock poured out of the volcano. This caused rivers to flood. Four states were covered with ash. More than sixty people were killed.

4. Ching and her mother were shopping for groceries. While they were waiting at the checkout line, her mother realized she had forgotten something. She turned to Ching and asked, "Could you go get me some eggs, please?" Ching ran to get the eggs. As she was coming back, she did not notice the wet floor.

5. Marta and her cousin Pilar set up a lawn-mowing service. They had made quite a bit of money over the summer. Mr. Lee was their neighbor. He had been sick lately, and his lawn had not been mowed. Marta and Pilar decided to mow the lawn for him. When Mr. Lee offered to pay them, they wouldn't take his money.

SCORE

Fact	Inference	
○	○	**1. A.** The moon is coldest during lunar night.
○	○	**B.** Lunar night lasts two weeks.
○	○	**C.** The moon is hotter and colder than Earth.
○	○	**D.** It is hottest on the moon at noon.

Fact	Inference	
○	○	**2. A.** The horses were thirsty.
○	○	**B.** Miguel was excited about going to the rodeo.
○	○	**C.** Ravon drove up in a truck.
○	○	**D.** Miguel did not finish his work.

Fact	Inference	
○	○	**3. A.** Mount St. Helens erupted in 1980.
○	○	**B.** The volcano did not erupt often.
○	○	**C.** People lived near Mount St. Helens.
○	○	**D.** Mount St. Helens is in Washington.

Fact	Inference	
○	○	**4. A.** Ching fell down on the floor.
○	○	**B.** Someone had spilled water on the floor.
○	○	**C.** Ching's mother asked her to get eggs.
○	○	**D.** Ching was a helpful girl.

Fact	Inference	
○	○	**5. A.** Marta and Pilar wanted to help Mr. Lee.
○	○	**B.** Mr. Lee had been sick lately.
○	○	**C.** Marta and Pilar were hard workers.
○	○	**D.** Mr. Lee offered to pay the girls.

1. The moon was full. The sea air smelled fresh and clean. Sue and her mom decided to take a walk. Sue pushed her mom's wheelchair along the sidewalk. They could see the ocean in the distance. They stopped often to look up at the stars. The last few days of getting ready for their vacation had been very busy. Now it was time to have fun.

2. Popcorn is one of the oldest kinds of corn. It was first grown by people in North and South America. Today most popcorn is grown in Nebraska and Indiana.

3. Beth loved computers. Once or twice a week, she went to the computer store near her house. The owner was glad to let Beth use the computers, but he told her not to bring drinks inside. One day Beth carried a can of apple juice into the store.

4. Mammoths lived thousands of years ago. They looked a little like elephants. They had trunks and long teeth called tusks. Some had hair all over their bodies. They were called woolly mammoths. The bones of mammoths have been found in Siberia. The last mammoths died about ten thousand years ago.

5. Sean and Matt were friends. They had been practicing for the school play. They both wanted to play the part of Robin Hood. When Mrs. Gray called the list of actors, Sean found out that Matt would get to play Robin Hood. Sean didn't play with Matt after school that day. He stayed alone in his room.

Fact	Inference		
○	○	**1.**	**A.** Sue and her mom were on vacation.
○	○		**B.** It was night.
○	○		**C.** Sue and her mom liked being together.
○	○		**D.** The stars were bright.

Fact	Inference		
○	○	**2.**	**A.** Popcorn is grown in Indiana.
○	○		**B.** People in South America grew popcorn.
○	○		**C.** Popcorn doesn't grow well everywhere.
○	○		**D.** People still eat popcorn.

Fact	Inference		
○	○	**3.**	**A.** Beth spilled the apple juice.
○	○		**B.** The owner was angry with Beth.
○	○		**C.** Beth liked apple juice.
○	○		**D.** The store was near Beth's house.

Fact	Inference		
○	○	**4.**	**A.** Woolly mammoths had hair on their bodies.
○	○		**B.** Mammoths had trunks and tusks.
○	○		**C.** Woolly mammoths died long ago.
○	○		**D.** Mammoths lived in Siberia.

Fact	Inference		
○	○	**5.**	**A.** Sean wanted to play Robin Hood.
○	○		**B.** Matt was a better actor than Sean.
○	○		**C.** Sean was sad he didn't get the part.
○	○		**D.** Matt got the part of Robin Hood.

1. Andy watched his mother take his training wheels off. He was excited to try out his bike. But without the training wheels, he kept falling over. Then his older brother Jeff came outside. Jeff had an idea. He ran beside Andy as Andy pedaled the bike. Andy rode faster and faster. Soon Jeff couldn't keep up. Andy was riding the bike by himself!

2. Mushrooms grow under piles of fallen leaves or on dead logs. People eat mushrooms in spaghetti or on pizza, but not all mushrooms are good to eat. Some mushrooms have poison in them. The poisonous ones are called toadstools.

3. Maggie, Lauren, and Sandra were playing basketball. Lauren ran down the court, bouncing the ball. As she tried to shoot a basket, Maggie pushed the ball away. It bounced off the court and hit a parked car nearby. The ball smashed the car's back window. Maggie began running away. "Let's get out of here!" she yelled to her friends.

4. What happens if the arm of a starfish gets cut off? It grows a new one! The body of a starfish is shaped like a star. Each point is an arm. A starfish has eyes and feet on its arms. Its eyes are little spots on the end of its arms. The feet of a starfish are like tiny tubes under each arm.

5. The Jesse White Tumblers perform shows all over the country. Children from housing projects in Chicago make up the team. A housing project is a group of apartments for people without jobs or much money. The team has about 75 members. To stay on the team, they have to keep up their work at school.

Fact	Inference		
○	○	**1.**	**A.** Andy fell off his bike.
○	○		**B.** Jeff wanted to help Andy.
○	○		**C.** Andy's mother took off his training wheels.
○	○		**D.** Jeff was Andy's older brother.

Fact	Inference		
○	○	**2.**	**A.** Some mushrooms are poisonous.
○	○		**B.** People eat mushrooms on pizza.
○	○		**C.** Mushrooms grow on dead logs.
○	○		**D.** People should not eat toadstools.

Fact	Inference		
○	○	**3.**	**A.** Maggie was afraid.
○	○		**B.** The ball smashed the window.
○	○		**C.** Maggie didn't plan to hit the car.
○	○		**D.** Lauren and Sandra didn't follow Maggie.

Fact	Inference		
○	○	**4.**	**A.** A starfish has feet.
○	○		**B.** Starfish can grow new arms.
○	○		**C.** A starfish can see.
○	○		**D.** Starfish are shaped like stars.

Fact	Inference		
○	○	**5.**	**A.** The Jesse White Tumblers are famous.
○	○		**B.** The team members don't have much money.
○	○		**C.** People live in housing projects.
○	○		**D.** There are 75 members on the team.

1. Ted had been sick for a week. He had chicken pox. His teacher asked if anyone in the class could take Ted's homework to him. Dave had already had chicken pox, so he raised his hand. On his way to Ted's house, he bought some baseball cards for Ted.

2. People have used wheels for over five thousand years. They were probably first used in Middle Eastern countries. Chinese people learned to use the wheel about two thousand years later. Indians in North and South America did not use wheels for work at that time. But they did put wheels on their toys.

3. "Come right home after school," Ann's mom told her. "I will," said Ann. She waved goodbye and rode off on her bike to school. On her way home, Ann saw some of her friends at the park. They were riding their bikes through a mud puddle. It looked like fun. Ann decided to join them.

4. Gold was found in Georgia many years ago. At that time mostly Cherokee Indians lived there. White settlers wanted the gold and the land. With the help of the United States government, they forced the Cherokees to move west. Thousands of Cherokees died on the march to Oklahoma. It was called the Trail of Tears.

5. Luke and Tom wanted to make cookies. Tom's mother helped them get started. But then she went outside to work in the yard. "Take the cookies out in ten minutes," she said. The boys carefully put the cookies in the oven. Then they went outside to play with Tom's new puppy. They were having so much fun that they forgot about the cookies.

Fact	Inference	
○	○	**1. A.** Dave and Ted were friends.
○	○	**B.** Ted had chicken pox.
○	○	**C.** Dave raised his hand.
○	○	**D.** Ted liked baseball cards.

Fact	Inference	
○	○	**2. A.** Some Native American toys had wheels.
○	○	**B.** People in China used wheels to do work.
○	○	**C.** China is not in the Middle East.
○	○	**D.** Wheels have been used for a long time.

Fact	Inference	
○	○	**3. A.** Ann rode her bike to school.
○	○	**B.** Ann was late getting home.
○	○	**C.** Ann's friends were at the park.
○	○	**D.** Ann did not obey her mother.

Fact	Inference	
○	○	**4. A.** Gold was found in Georgia.
○	○	**B.** The settlers wanted the land.
○	○	**C.** The march to Oklahoma was long.
○	○	**D.** The Cherokees were forced to move west.

Fact	Inference	
○	○	**5. A.** Tom's mother went to work in the yard.
○	○	**B.** The boys played with Tom's puppy.
○	○	**C.** Luke and Tom were having fun.
○	○	**D.** The cookies burned.

1. One man made a pizza so big it could feed thirty thousand people. The pizza was over one hundred feet across. It was cut into over ninety thousand slices! The man's name was Mr. Avato. He set a world record.

2. "Don't you ever come here again!" Kim shouted to her best friend Gail. "Don't you worry. I won't!" Gail shouted back. Gail slammed the front door shut as she left. After a few minutes, Kim was sorry for what she had said. She ran out the front door and headed toward Gail's house. Gail was running down the sidewalk to Kim's house.

3. Have you ever wondered what it would be like to live in another country? Each year thousands of American students do just that. They live in another country for a few months. Some even stay for a year. They live with a host family in the new country. The host family members try to make the student a part of their family life. The students go to school, make friends, visit new places, and eat new foods. Sometimes they even learn to speak another language.

4. Rob heard a rooster crow. He opened his eyes and felt the sun shining through the window. It was his first day on his cousin's farm. He jumped out of bed and began putting on his jeans. When his aunt called him to breakfast, he ran downstairs eagerly.

5. Ty Cobb was one of baseball's greatest players. He played for 24 years with the Detroit Tigers and Philadelphia Athletics. They called him the Georgia Peach. He was in more games and batted more times than anyone else in major league baseball.

Fact	Inference	
○	○	**1.** **A.** The pizza was over 100 feet across.
○	○	**B.** The pizza set a world record.
○	○	**C.** Mr. Avato likes pizza.
○	○	**D.** There were over ninety thousand pieces.

Fact	Inference	
○	○	**2.** **A.** Kim and Gail were best friends.
○	○	**B.** Gail was coming to say she was sorry.
○	○	**C.** Kim shouted at Gail.
○	○	**D.** Gail slammed the front door.

Fact	Inference	
○	○	**3.** **A.** Most host families speak English.
○	○	**B.** Some students learn a new language.
○	○	**C.** Host families like Americans.
○	○	**D.** The students visit new places.

Fact	Inference	
○	○	**4.** **A.** Rob liked farm life.
○	○	**B.** The sun was shining.
○	○	**C.** Rob was hungry.
○	○	**D.** A rooster crowed.

Fact	Inference	
○	○	**5.** **A.** Ty Cobb was from Georgia.
○	○	**B.** Ty Cobb was a great baseball player.
○	○	**C.** Sports fans liked Ty Cobb.
○	○	**D.** Ty Cobb made a lot of money.

1. Jan heard someone crying for help. She ran down toward the lake. A boy was splashing around wildly. In a flash Jan ran to get the rope that hung on a tree nearby. She threw it once, but the boy missed it. She walked a little ways into the cold water and tried again. This time she could feel the boy pull on the other end.

2. No one really knows what happened to the first English settlers in the New World. Their leader, John White, left them to go to England for supplies. When he returned over a year later, the settlers were gone. Some people think they were killed. Others think they may have gone to live with a friendly Native American tribe. We will probably never solve the mystery of the "Lost Colony."

3. It was a warm, windy day. Tina and Sam went to fly their kite. "Find a good spot this time," their mother said. "Remember what happened when you flew your kite over by the woods." But the open field was very far away, and Tina and Sam were in a hurry. They walked toward the woods.

4. The Eagles were tied with the Wildcats. There were only three seconds left in the game. The Eagles' best player had the ball. He bounced it once before he jumped up to make the shot. Everyone was quiet as they watched the ball fly toward the basket. Then the Eagle fans jumped up and yelled, "All right!"

5. Sally Ride was the first American woman to travel in space. In 1983 she made a flight that lasted six days. The flight was made on the space shuttle *Challenger*. The next year she made another flight. She studied Earth's weather.

Fact	Inference	
○	○	**1. A.** Jan saved the boy.
○	○	**B.** The boy was drowning in the lake.
○	○	**C.** Jan knew where a rope was.
○	○	**D.** Jan heard someone crying for help.

Fact	Inference	
○	○	**2. A.** The settlers needed supplies.
○	○	**B.** John White was the leader of the group.
○	○	**C.** Some people think the settlers were killed.
○	○	**D.** No one really knows what happened.

Fact	Inference	
○	○	**3. A.** Tina and Sam went to fly a kite.
○	○	**B.** Windy days are good for flying kites.
○	○	**C.** Tina and Sam were in a hurry.
○	○	**D.** Last time their kite got stuck in a tree.

Fact	Inference	
○	○	**4. A.** The Eagles were a basketball team.
○	○	**B.** The score was tied.
○	○	**C.** The Eagles won the game.
○	○	**D.** There were three seconds left in the game.

Fact	Inference	
○	○	**5. A.** Sally Ride traveled in space.
○	○	**B.** The *Challenger* was a space shuttle.
○	○	**C.** Sally Ride was interested in science.
○	○	**D.** Sally Ride studied the weather.

1. The Vikings were probably first to find North America. Ruins of Viking houses have been found in Newfoundland. Their houses were built around A.D. 1000. English fishers probably didn't reach that area until 1481. Columbus thought he was the first one to find the New World in 1492.

2. George hated playing softball. One by one his friends had been picked for a team. Everyone's name had been called except for Mike's and his. Mike was chosen next. George couldn't stand it any longer. He ran back to the school building and slammed the door behind him.

3. Sitting Bull was born in South Dakota. He became a Sioux chief. It was a very hard time for his people. White settlers were moving onto his land. In 1868 the United States asked the Sioux and Cheyenne chiefs to sign a peace treaty. Many chiefs signed the treaty and lived on the reservation. But Sitting Bull did not. He wanted to live the old way.

4. When we think of windmills, we often think of Holland. The people there used windmills to take water off their land. That way they had more land for farming. Now windmills are used to make electricity.

5. "Don't forget to take your library books back today," Liz's mother told her. But the books stayed in Liz's room for two more weeks. By the time Liz saw them again, she owed a big fine. She didn't want to tell her mother about it, but she didn't have the money to pay the fine. That afternoon she found a purse on the floor of the school bus. Inside was a five-dollar bill.

Fact	Inference	
○	○	**1.** **A.** Vikings built houses about A.D. 1000.
○	○	**B.** Newfoundland is in North America.
○	○	**C.** Columbus didn't reach the New World first.
○	○	**D.** Columbus didn't know about the Vikings.

Fact	Inference	
○	○	**2.** **A.** George was not good at softball.
○	○	**B.** George felt sad that he was chosen last.
○	○	**C.** George ran back to the school building.
○	○	**D.** George slammed the door.

Fact	Inference	
○	○	**3.** **A.** Sitting Bull was a Sioux chief.
○	○	**B.** Sitting Bull did not like the white settlers.
○	○	**C.** Sitting Bull did not sign the treaty.
○	○	**D.** Sitting Bull did not want to change.

Fact	Inference	
○	○	**4.** **A.** There is not enough farmland in Holland.
○	○	**B.** Farmland must be fairly dry.
○	○	**C.** Holland has many windmills.
○	○	**D.** Now windmills make electricity.

Fact	Inference	
○	○	**5.** **A.** Liz did not have money to pay the fine.
○	○	**B.** Liz was afraid her mother would be angry.
○	○	**C.** Liz found a purse.
○	○	**D.** Liz used the money to pay her fine.

1. The English Channel flows between France and England. At least 228 people have swum the 21-mile crossing. Some crossings may have been in secret. Police think a French soldier crossed the channel in 1815. He escaped from a prison in Dover, England.

2. Pam was in the hospital. Her class wanted to show Pam that they missed her. "I have an idea," Emily said. "Let's make a big banner for Pam." The class spent the morning making the banner. It said "The kids at Brook School care about you!" They asked other students in the school to sign it, too.

3. Did you ever hear of the Underground Railroad? It wasn't a real railroad. But it did carry slaves to their freedom. It was run by people like Harriet Tubman. She had once been a slave, too. Slaves who were running away were told about safe places to stay. Harriet Tubman helped over three hundred slaves escape to freedom.

4. Alex's dad had lost his job. His family did not have much money. One afternoon Alex and his dad were walking near their home. Alex ran ahead to see a squirrel. Then suddenly he saw something under a leaf. He pulled it out and saw that it was a twenty-dollar bill. Alex thought of all the things he would like to buy. But he turned around. "Come here, Dad," he said.

5. Henry Ford was one of America's first carmakers. He found ways to make cars cost less. Many people couldn't buy other cars, which cost more. But most Americans had enough money to buy Ford's Model T. The Ford Motor Company sold 15 million Model T's in less than 20 years.

Fact	Inference	
○	○	**1. A.** A soldier escaped from prison.
○	○	**B.** The channel is filled with water.
○	○	**C.** The prison was near the channel.
○	○	**D.** The channel is 21 miles wide.

Fact	Inference	
○	○	**2. A.** Pam needed to be cheered up.
○	○	**B.** The students made a banner.
○	○	**C.** Emily took the banner to Pam.
○	○	**D.** The students signed the banner.

Fact	Inference	
○	○	**3. A.** Slaves were told about safe places to stay.
○	○	**B.** Harriet Tubman was once a slave.
○	○	**C.** People didn't like being slaves.
○	○	**D.** Harriet Tubman cared about slaves.

Fact	Inference	
○	○	**4. A.** Alex gave his dad the money.
○	○	**B.** The money was under a leaf.
○	○	**C.** Alex wanted to help his father.
○	○	**D.** Alex's dad had lost his job.

Fact	Inference	
○	○	**5. A.** Other cars cost more than the Model T.
○	○	**B.** Henry Ford was a smart businessperson.
○	○	**C.** Fifteen million Model T's were sold.
○	○	**D.** Americans liked Model T's.

1. The Venus's flytrap is a strange plant. An insect that flies near it doesn't have much of a chance. When an insect touches the leaves in the center of the plant, the leaves snap shut. The insect gets trapped inside. It takes a few days for the Venus's flytrap to finish eating the insect.

2. Ben and his dad were out running. Suddenly there was a loud crack of thunder. Ben's dad said, "We'd better head toward home." Light rain started to fall. "Faster, son," he said. The rain began coming down harder. Ben and his dad were getting soaked. Then a blue van came around the corner. "Mom!" Ben called out.

3. Koko was a gorilla. Penny, her owner, had taught the ape sign language. One day Penny asked Koko what she wanted for her birthday. "Cat," Koko answered. Penny bought a toy cat for Koko. But when Koko opened her present, she threw it down. Koko had wanted a real cat. A few months later, Penny gave Koko a real cat. Then Koko was happy.

4. Dean's grandmother was in the hospital. Dean and his mom had planned to visit her on Saturday afternoon. On Friday a friend called Dean. He asked if Dean would like to go skating Saturday afternoon. Dean loved to skate. But he told his friend that he would go skating some other time.

5. The summer night was warm and peaceful. Zack and his dad lay in their sleeping bags. They stared up at the sky together. The stars were bright. An owl hooted not far away. After a while Zack turned on his side. He went to sleep thinking about the great day it had been.

Fact	Inference	
○	○	**1. A.** A Venus's flytrap is a plant.
○	○	**B.** The Venus's flytrap's leaves snap shut.
○	○	**C.** The leaves trap the insect.
○	○	**D.** Venus's flytraps eat insects.

Fact	Inference	
○	○	**2. A.** Ben and his dad enjoyed running together.
○	○	**B.** Ben's mom knew they were out running.
○	○	**C.** It was raining hard.
○	○	**D.** Ben was glad to see his mom.

Fact	Inference	
○	○	**3. A.** Penny was Koko's owner.
○	○	**B.** Koko wanted a cat for her birthday.
○	○	**C.** The real cat made Koko happy.
○	○	**D.** Koko was upset when she didn't get a cat.

Fact	Inference	
○	○	**4. A.** Dean cared about his grandmother.
○	○	**B.** Dean loved to skate.
○	○	**C.** A friend called Dean.
○	○	**D.** Dean's grandmother was sick.

Fact	Inference	
○	○	**5. A.** Zack had a great day.
○	○	**B.** Zack's dad took him camping.
○	○	**C.** The stars were bright.
○	○	**D.** Zack went to sleep.

1. Tanya and Margo had gone to the same school for five years. One day Margo noticed that Tanya looked sad. "What's the matter?" Margo asked. "Oh, I can't believe it!" Tanya said. "My dad got a new job in Boston. We're moving next month."

2. A coral reef is a strange and beautiful place. It has towers, tunnels, caves, and castles. But it is under the sea. The coral is made of shells from tiny animals. It looks like rock. Different kinds of fish swim around the reef. They make the reef look like a rainbow of color.

3. Kurt had taken piano lessons for the past year. Now it was the night of the spring program. Kurt hoped that his time would never come. But finally his teacher came to tell him he was next. Kurt walked on the stage. After a few minutes of playing, he stood up while the people clapped. He had played his song perfectly!

4. One of the first computers was called ENIAC. It was built in 1946. It could do about five thousand math problems in a second. Today's computers are much smaller and faster than the early ones.

5. Dodo birds once lived on some islands in the Indian Ocean. They were about the same size as a turkey. Dodos could not fly. They had a hooked beak, short legs, and a short neck. Dodo eggs were eaten by other animals on the islands. The last dodos died out over two hundred years ago.

Fact	Inference		
○	○	**1.** **A.**	Tanya didn't want to move to Boston.
○	○	**B.**	The girls had been friends for years.
○	○	**C.**	Tanya looked sad.
○	○	**D.**	Tanya's dad got a new job.

Fact	Inference		
○	○	**2.** **A.**	Coral reefs are beautiful.
○	○	**B.**	Fish swim around a coral reef.
○	○	**C.**	The fish are colorful.
○	○	**D.**	A coral reef is made of shells.

Fact	Inference		
○	○	**3.** **A.**	Kurt was nervous before the program.
○	○	**B.**	Kurt played his song perfectly.
○	○	**C.**	The piano was on stage.
○	○	**D.**	Kurt had taken piano lessons for a year.

Fact	Inference		
○	○	**4.** **A.**	ENIAC was one of the first computers.
○	○	**B.**	Computers today are smaller than ENIAC.
○	○	**C.**	ENIAC was built in 1946.
○	○	**D.**	Computers work faster than people do.

Fact	Inference		
○	○	**5.** **A.**	A dodo was the size of a turkey.
○	○	**B.**	The dodos died two hundred years ago.
○	○	**C.**	A dodo was larger than a chicken.
○	○	**D.**	Other animals ate dodo eggs.

Think and Apply

What's Next?

Read the following pairs of sentences. Then decide what will happen next. Write your answer for each item on the line below the sentences. The first one is done for you.

1. The air inside the hot-air balloon is heated.
   The pilot gets into the basket.

   The balloon rises, and the pilot takes a ride.

2. The hungry eagle flies across the sky.
   A rabbit runs across the ground.

   _____

3. Clouds darken the sky.
   Thunder is heard, and lightning is seen.

   _____

4. Amy fills a bowl with cat food.
   The cat comes in from the other room.

   _____

5. Carlos takes out his paints and a paintbrush.
   He puts a sheet of paper on the table.

   _____

6. The movie ends.
   The lights come on in the theater.

   _____

7. Kate is walking to school.
   She feels a rock in her shoe.

   _____

Getting to Know You

Read each story. Think about each person in the story. Then look at the words in the boxes below. If a word tells about that person, write **yes** in the box. If a word does not tell about the person, write **no**.

Story 1   Jake and Tom were going outside to play. Jake saw his little sister Gail. She was crying. Tom told Jake not to worry about Gail. He wanted Jake to play with him. But Jake asked Gail what the problem was. Gail explained that her kitten had climbed up a tree and was too afraid to come down. Jake told Gail not to cry. Then he ran into the house. A minute later he returned with a backpack. Tom told Jake he wasn't going to wait any longer, and he left. Jake smiled at Gail. Then he carefully climbed the tree, placed the kitten in the backpack, and climbed back down. Gail hugged her big brother and her little kitten.

	kind	gentle	selfish
Tom			
Jake			

Story 2   Sally woke up. She saw she had forgotten to set her alarm again. Sally knew she was going to be late for work. She got dressed and ran out the door. She yelled hello to her neighbors as she ran to the bus stop. She hoped she would get to work on time tomorrow.

	friendly	sick	forgetful
Sally			

To check your answers, turn to page 62.

Tell Me Why

Read each story. Then read the question that follows it. Write your answers on the lines below each question.

1. It had not rained for a long time, and the pond had dried up. The rancher knew he would have to do something soon or his cattle would die. One day he had a great idea. He burned the needles off some prickly pear cactus. The cattle ate the juicy cactus plants. The rancher knew he had saved his cattle.

Why did the cattle eat the cactus?

_____

_____

_____

2. Bill dressed in some big, colorful clothes and large shoes. Then he put on his make-up and green hair. He popped on his big, red nose. Now Bill was ready to go to work.

Why did Bill wear a costume to work?

_____

_____

_____

3. The frog sat on a log. A fly buzzed close by. The frog sat very still. The fly came a little closer. Suddenly the frog stuck out its tongue.

Why did the frog stick out its tongue?

_____

_____

_____

To check your answers, turn to page 62.

Check Yourself

Unit 1 pp. 6-7	Unit 2 pp. 8-9	Unit 3 pp. 10-11	Unit 4 pp. 12-13	Unit 5 pp. 14-15	Unit 6 pp. 16-17	Unit 7 pp. 18-19	Unit 8 pp. 20-21
1. A	1. C	1. A	1. B	1. A	1. C	1. A	1. B
2. C	2. A	2. B	2. A	2. C	2. B	2. B	2. D
3. B	3. B	3. A	3. C	3. D	3. D	3. D	3. D
4. D	4. B	4. D	4. D	4. D	4. A	4. C	4. A
5. B	5. D	5. C	5. C	5. B	5. B	5. A	5. C

Unit 9 pp. 22-23	Unit 10 pp. 24-25	Unit 11 pp. 26-27	Unit 12 pp. 28-29	Unit 13 pp. 30-31	Unit 14 pp. 32-33	Unit 15 pp. 34-35	Unit 16 pp. 36-37
1. C	1. B	1. A	1. B	1.	1.	1.	1.
				A. F	A. I	A. F	A. I
				B. I	B. F	B. I	B. F
				C. I	C. F	C. F	C. F
				D. F	D. I	D. I	D. I
2. A	2. A	2. D	2. C	2.	2.	2.	2.
				A. F	A. I	A. F	A. I
				B. F	B. I	B. I	B. F
				C. I	C. I	C. F	C. F
				D. F	D. F	D. I	D. I
3. D	3. D	3. C	3. A	3.	3.	3.	3.
				A. I	A. I	A. F	A. F
				B. F	B. F	B. I	B. I
				C. F	C. I	C. F	C. I
4. B	4. C	4. C	4. B	D. I	D. F	D. F	D. F
				4.	4.	4.	4.
				A. F	A. F	A. I	A. I
				B. I	B. I	B. F	B. I
				C. F	C. I	C. I	C. F
5. A	5. A	5. B	5. D	D. F	D. F	D. F	D. I
				5.	5.	5.	5.
				A. F	A. F	A. I	A. I
				B. I	B. F	B. I	B. F
				C. F	C. F	C. I	C. I
				D. I	D. I	D. F	D. F

Unit **17** pp.38-39	Unit **18** pp. 40-41	Unit **19** pp. 42-43	Unit **20** pp. 44-45	Unit **21** pp. 46-47	Unit **22** pp. 48-49	Unit **23** pp. 50-51	Unit **24** pp. 52-53	Unit **25** pp. 54-55
1.	**1.**	**1.**	**1.**	**1.**	**1.**	**1.**	**1.**	**1.**
A. I	A. F	A. I	A. F	A. I	A. F	A. F	A. F	A. I
B. I	B. I	B. F	B. F	B. I	B. I	B. I	B. F	B. I
C. I	C. F	C. F	C. I	C. I	C. I	C. I	C. F	C. F
D. I	D. F	D. I	D. F	D. F	D. I	D. F	D. F	D. F
2.	**2.**	**2.**	**2.**	**2.**	**2.**	**2.**	**2.**	**2.**
A. F	A. F	A. F	A. F	A. I	A. I	A. I	A. I	A. F
B. F	B. F	B. I	B. I	B. F	B. I	B. F	B. I	B. F
C. I	C. F	C. I	C. F	C. F	C. F	C. I	C. I	C. I
D. I	D. I	D. F	D. F	D. F	D. F	D. I	D. I	D. F
3.	**3.**	**3.**	**3.**	**3.**	**3.**	**3.**	**3.**	**3.**
A. I	A. I	A. F	A. I	A. F	A. F	A. F	A. F	A. I
B. I	B. F	B. I	B. F	B. I	B. I	B. F	B. F	B. F
C. I	C. I	C. F	C. I	C. F	C. F	C. I	C. F	C. I
D. F	D. I	D. I	D. F	D. I	D. I	D. I	D. I	D. F
4.	**4.**	**4.**	**4.**	**4.**	**4.**	**4.**	**4.**	**4.**
A. F	A. F	A. F	A. I	A. I	A. I	A. I	A. I	A. F
B. F	B. F	B. F	B. F	B. F	B. I	B. F	B. F	B. F
C. F	C. I	C. I	C. I	C. I	C. I	C. I	C. F	C. F
D. I	D. F	D. F	D. F	D. F	D. F	D. F	D. I	D. I
5.	**5.**	**5.**	**5.**	**5.**	**5.**	**5.**	**5.**	**5.**
A. F	A. I	A. F	A. I	A. F	A. F	A. F	A. F	A. F
B. I	B. I	B. F	B. F	B. F	B. I	B. I	B. I	B. F
C. I	C. F	C. F	C. I	C. I	C. F	C. F	C. F	C. I
D. F	D. F	D. I	D. I	D. F	D. I	D. I	D. F	D. F

Practice Making Inferences, Page 3
2. C

More Practice Making Inferences, Page 4
2. A. F
   B. F
   C. I
   D. F

What's Next? Page 56
2. The hungry eagle catches and eats the rabbit.
3. There is a storm.
4. The cat eats the food in its bowl.
5. Carlos paints a picture.
6. The people leave the theater.
7. Kate stops to take the rock out of her shoe.

Getting to Know You, Page 57
Story 1:

	kind	gentle	selfish
Tom	no	no	yes
Jake	yes	yes	no

Story 2:

	friendly	sick	forgetful
Sally	yes	no	yes

Tell Me Why, Page 58
1. The cattle were thirsty, and the cactus contained water.
2. Bill worked as a clown.
3. The frog wanted to catch and eat the fly.